HUME IN 90 MINUTES

Paul Strathern

HUME
(1711–76)
in 90 minutes

Constable · London

First published in Great Britain 1996
by Constable and Company Limited
3 The Lanchesters, 162 Fulham Palace Road
London W6 9ER
Copyright © Paul Strathern 1996
The right of Paul Strathern to be identified as author
of this work has been asserted by him
in accordance with the Copyright,
Designs and Patents Act 1988
ISBN 0 09 475950 2
Set in Linotron Sabon by
Rowland Phototypesetting Ltd,
Bury St Edmunds, Suffolk
Printed in Great Britain by
St Edmundsbury Press Ltd,
Bury St Edmunds, Suffolk

A CIP catalogue record of this book
is available from the British Library

All translations are by the author.

Contents

Introduction and background to the philosophy

Before Hume, philosophers were often accused of being atheists. Hume was the first one who admitted it.

Being judged an atheist was not an enviable accolade for philosophers, or anyone else. Society had a way of dealing with such unorthodox thinkers – from Ancient Greece (poison) to the Middle Ages (Inquisition). Philosophers thus went to great lengths to convince everybody (and themselves) that they were not atheists. Hume's admission of theological bankruptcy was treated as a public scandal – but attempts to dissuade him were made with philosophical argument, rather than the rack. This says as much for the tolerance of eighteenth-century British society as it does for Hume. Yet if he wished to remain consistent with his philosophy, Hume could have taken no other stance.

Philosophy was a long time coming to this. Several philosophers of the ancient world – such as some Stoics and a few Cynics – were close to it. But Socrates was sentenced to death for not respecting the gods, and in Ancient Rome it was often impossible not to believe in God (especially when he was also the emperor). Thus faith became essential – for those who wished to continue thinking, just as much for those who wished to continue at all.

Early in the Christian era philosophy was swallowed whole by theology. Plato and Aristotle became the Holy Writ, and philosophy consisted largely of elaborations on such accepted texts. These were followed by elaborations on the elaborations, and much heroic work rendering these elaborations acceptable to Christian dogma. A sideline developed with the misuse of logic in trying to prove the existence of God. A certain amount of all this activity was extremely ingenious, and even creative. But it was not original. The basic assumptions were always the same.

These assumptions were first seriously questioned in the sixteenth century by Descartes, who is now regarded as the founder of modern philosophy. Descartes swept aside the old assumptions and based his philosophy upon reason. By a process of rational doubt, he showed that it is possible to deny everything – with one exception. I cannot doubt everything and yet at the same time doubt that I am thinking. 'I think therefore I am' was his celebrated conclusion. Thus Descartes reached the bedrock upon which he built the rational structure of his philosophy.

Just half a century later, the British philosopher John Locke went one step further with the introduction of empiricism. This claimed the ultimate bedrock of philosophy lay not in reason, but in experience. In Locke's view, all that we know is gained ultimately from experience. We have no innate ideas – just sensations, and the ideas we gain from reflecting on these sensations. It looked as if philosophy had reached its ultimate limit.

But it wasn't long before someone took this one step further. The British empirical tradition took a step over the edge of sanity with the arrival of the Irishman Berkeley. If our knowledge of the world is based only on our experience, how can we know that the world exists when we're not perceiving it? The world was thus reduced to a figment, and philosophy to a laughing stock. But fortunately for the world, Berkeley was a bishop and a God-fearing man. Of course the world continued to exist, he declared, even when no one was perceiving it. How could this be? Because the world was always being perceived by God.

This philosophical sleight of hand saved Berkeley a lot of trouble (and not only with his archbishop and his congregation). The world now had a prop. This was to last just thirty years, until Hume entered the fray.

Life and work

Hume is the only philosopher whose ideas remain plausible to us today. The Ancient Greeks are readable as high literature, but their philosophy seems like brilliant fairytales. The medievalism of Augustine and Aquinas are alien to the modern sensibility. Descartes and the rationalists make us realize that the human condition is not rational; the earlier empiricists seem either self-evident, wrong-headed or absurd. And the philosophers after Hume mostly fall into either of the last two categories.

What I have just tried to do, Hume succeeded in doing – he reduced philosophy to ruins. Hume went one step further even than Berkeley, and thought the empirical situation through to its logical conclusion. He denied the existence of everything – except our actual perceptions themselves. In doing this, he placed us in a difficult position. This is solipsism: I alone exist, and the world is nothing more than part of my consciousness. Here we arrive at the endgame of philosophy: one from which it's impossible to escape. Checkmate.

Then suddenly we realize that this doesn't matter. Regardless of what the philosophers say, the world remains there – we still go on as before. As did Hume: whose gargantuan frame and ready wit were not that of a bewildered Beckett-like solipsist thinking himself to bits. What Hume expressed was the *status* of our knowledge about the world. Neither the world of religion nor the world of science are certain. We can choose to believe in religion if we wish, but we do so on no certain evidence. And we can choose to make scientific deductions in order to impose our will upon the world. But neither religion nor science exists in itself. Both are merely our reactions to experience, one of any number of possible reactions.

Hume was descended from an auld Scots

family. His biography by E. C. Mossner includes a family tree tracing his ancestors back to the Home of Home, who died in 1424. The philosopher's later ancestors include a number of unappealing but apparently distinguished Scottish names, such as a Belcher of Tofts, a Home of Blackadder and a Norvell of Boghall. (A branch of the family was later to produce Britain's most risible post-war prime minister.)

David Hume was born on 24 April 1711 in Edinburgh. His father died when he was three. A remarkably high proportion of the major philosophers lost their fathers at an early age, and this has produced the usual psychological theories. The gist of these is that the lack of a male parental figure creates a profound need for certainty. This in turn causes the bereft son to create an abstract system that takes the place of the 'abstracted' father. Such psychological theories can be extremely brilliant, entertaining, and possibly even informative (though about what, I'm not quite sure.) In other words their resemblance to the philosophers they describe is uncanny in many aspects – except that of intellectual rigour.

By the time David Hume arrived on the scene, his branch of the distinguished family tree had descended to the point where it was living on the chilly little estate of Ninewells. This was nine miles west of Berwick-upon-Tweed near the village of Chirnside on the Scottish border. The original house where the philosopher grew up no longer exists, but the gullible philosophic tourist is shown the 'Philosopher's cave', down the slope to the south-east of the present house. This dank cramped uninviting aperture is where Hume is said to have meditated as a young lad, as well as during his later years (when its inner reaches might have proved something of a tight fit for his ample form.) If our thought is affected by our surroundings we would expect Hume's meditations in this instance to have

produced a somewhat neolithic philosophy
with claustrophobic tendencies – and indeed
this is much how the great German philosophers of the next hundred years came to
regard Hume's work. This was inevitable, as
the Germans were intent upon constructing
vast philosophical systems – baroque palaces
of metaphysics, no less – and had no wish to
occupy the primitive philosophic cave which
Hume had bequeathed them. But alas, philosophy should not be confused with architec-
tural aspiration.

Hume was brought up by his uncle, the local
minister, who had succeeded the philosopher's
father as the laird of Ninewells. Conditions at
Ninewells would have appeared austere and
distinctly rural by modern standards: barefoot
servants; the lower floor of the building con-
taining the winter cowsheds and chicken runs;
a diet based heavily on oatmeal, porridge and
kale (a nourishing traditional broth, or a dis-
gusting watery cabbage soup, depending upon

your taste). But Hume didn't feel that his childhood was deprived, either at the time or later. He was educated in the local school-master's cottage with neighbouring village children, in the egalitarian Scottish tradition which for so long surpassed its counterpart south of the border. Then from the age of twelve to fifteen he went to Edinburgh University. (Such early entry to Edinburgh University was quite normal at the time.)

After this, Hume was expected to study law. But he was already inclined otherwise, and began reading voraciously over a wide range of subjects. Only with extreme reluctance did he devote any time at all to studying for the bar. This conflict continued for the next three years. But gradually Hume's reading began to concentrate more and more upon philosophy, until one day 'there seem'd to be open'd up to me a New Scene of Thought'. His philosophical ideas were beginning to crystallize, and he conceived of the idea of writing down a system. By now the law 'appear'd nauseous to me', and eventually he decided to give it up altogether.

This was no easy decision. It meant he was abandoning the chance of earning a professional living. The long inner struggle over this decision cost Hume dearly, and shortly afterwards he had a nervous breakdown.

Hume went back to Ninewells, but his recovery was only intermittent. Between bouts of depression, he continued excitedly pursuing his new ideas. The local physician was called in several times, and was of the opinion that Hume was suffering from 'the Disease of the Learned'. He prescribed 'a Course of Bitters & Anti-hysteric pills'. He also advised Hume to take 'an English Pint of Claret every day' and take regular exercise in the form of long rides on horseback.

Up until now, Hume had been tall and thin: a gawky fellow, with gangling limbs. Yet despite his regime of exercise, he now began putting on weight. On his daily rides out into the bare hilly countryside the horse grew thinner as its rider expanded – gradually becoming the portly figure he was to remain for the rest of his life. This suggests that Hume's troubles during this period may in part have been glandular.

Hume's recovery was only gradual, and may in fact never have been complete. Certain mysterious episodes during his later life suggest recurrent mental instability.

Hume had no wish to continue living with his mother at Ninewells for ever. In 1734 a friend of the family found him a job as a clerk to a shipping merchant in Bristol. His motives for taking this job were various. He certainly needed the money. He also understood that the job would involve foreign travel. This appealed to his sense of adventure, and he also felt it would be beneficial for his mental health.

There is strong evidence that this continued to worry him. On his way to Bristol, Hume passed through London. Here he composed a long letter to Dr Arbuthnott, one of the leading physicians of the day. In it, Hume does his best to describe his illness – though this description is severely hampered by the limited knowledge and inadequate concepts of the day. He describes his disease as 'this Distemper', and refers to his 'inflam'd Imaginations'. He says: 'I am continually fortifying myself with Reflections against Death, & Poverty, & Shame, & Pain, & all the other Calamities of Life.' After outlining the remedies prescribed by his physician, he passes inconsequentially to some philosophical reflections: 'I believe 'tis a certain fact that most of the Philosophers who have gone before us, have been overthrown by the greatness of their genius, & that little more is requir'd to make a man succeed in this Study than to throw off all Prejudices either for his own Opinions or for this of others.' Hume ends by asking various questions about his illness ('Whether I can hope for a Recovery?'), which he answers himself ('Assuredly you can'). And this appears to have done the trick. Hume never sent his ten-page letter (though he kept it all his life). He seems to have found that the mere writing of it was a cure in itself. Or at least as near a cure as he would ever find.

Hume now settled down to work in Bristol, and discovered that his job as a clerk was unlikely to involve any foreign travel. Relations with his employer gradually deteriorated, and eventually he left. By his twenty-fourth birthday he was back at Ninewells, where he began to get a bad name for his 'superior and irreligious ways'. By this stage Hume had inherited a small private income of forty pounds per annum, which enabled him to live frugally without employment.

He now set about writing down his philosophical observations, with the aim of creating a new philosophy which would make him famous. (Throughout his life Hume made little secret of his ultimate aim: 'my love of literary fame, my ruling passion'. Indeed, it was as a literary figure, more than as a philosopher, that Hume was to achieve fame. In later life, Boswell was to refer to him as 'the greatest writer in Britain', and to this day he is listed in the British Library catalogue as 'David Hume, the historian'.) After a few months Hume decided to set off for France. Here he could live well on his small private income, and in isolation he would be able to concentrate on his new philosophy without interruption or speculations of a more practical nature. (At Ninewells there was always Mother, and his uncle, neither of whom were philosophy fans.)

There is a story that Hume left Ninewells in a hurry. Not long after he went to France an unmarried young local woman called Agnes, who was said to have 'a bad record with such matters', announced that she was pregnant. The attitude towards this kind of thing in Scotland at the time was all very Christian. Poor deserted Agnes was exhibited at church, where the local minister (Hume's uncle) delivered the customary public denouncement, which ended with the pious hope that she would die in childbirth. As if this display of compassion and Christian love was not enough, Agnes was then hauled before the Sessions, where she almost certainly received a further punishment. Again, this probably involved some kind of public humiliation – always a favoured method of retribution in a hypocritical society. (I'm told that this is due to unconscious masochism: the thrill induced by the fact that *you* haven't yet been caught.) During the course of Agnes's examination at the sessions, she eventually named the father of her unborn child as the absent Hume – probably to protect the real father. This was the sessions' firm conviction, at any rate. We shall never know the truth.

With one notable exception, this is the main evidence we have of Hume's sexual inclinations. According to Mossner, Hume 'in later life, in Italy and France and Scotland, was to prove a man of normal sexual desires'. Since not much else is recorded about these normal sexual desires, one can only assume they were fulfilled by hospitality – with enthusiastic chambermaids and demanding hostesses. And since Hume is one of the few literary figures of the age who didn't catch the pox, it's unlikely that this hospitality was very frequent, or that he went with whores, who at the time were cheaper than hot-water bottles. (This latter is intended as a purely socio-economic observation, with no sexist undertones. These disease-ridden human hot-water bottles would in most cases have arrived at their condition after suffering the same fate as Agnes, victims of the hypocrisy so necessary to any upright society of closet masochists.)

Hume went first to live in Reims, but later moved to la Flèche, almost certainly because of its inspiring associations with Descartes, who had been educated here at the Jesuit college.

Within three years Hume had finished *A Treatise of Human Nature*. He was later to disparage this work, on account of what he considered to be its youthful extravagances. But he didn't disavow its philosophy – which contains almost all the original philosophical ideas for which he is today remembered. Bertrand Russell, in his *History of Western Philosophy*, is even of the view that this work contains the best parts of Hume's philosophy: some achievement for a man who was not yet thirty.

In *A Treatise of Human Nature* Hume attempted to define the basic principles of human knowledge. How do we know anything for certain? And what exactly is it that we do know for certain? In trying to answer these questions he followed in the empiricist tradition, believing that all our knowledge is ultimately based on experience. In Hume's view, experience consists of perceptions, of which there are two types: impressions and ideas. 'Those perceptions which enter with most force and violence we may name *impressions*; and, under this name, I comprehend all our sensations, passions and emotions, as they make their first appearance in the soul. By *ideas* I mean the faint images of these in thinking and reasoning.'

He explains: 'Every simple idea has a simple impression, which resembles it.' But we can also form complex ideas. These are derived from impressions, by way of simple ideas, but need not necessarily conform to an impression. For example, we can imagine a mermaid by combining our idea of a fish and our idea of a woman. By adhering strictly to this notion of impressions and ideas as the only certain basis for our knowledge, Hume arrives at some astonishing conclusions. Objects, continuity, the self, even cause and effect – all these are shown to be fallacious notions. We never actually experience an object – only impressions of its colour, shape, consistency, taste and so forth. Likewise, we have no actual impression that corresponds to continuity. Things simply happen one after another. We can't even say that one thing causes another to happen. We may observe one thing constantly following another (lit gunpowder, explosion) but there is no logical connection between the two, and no logical reason why they will happen in sequence in the future. 'We have no other notion of cause and effect, but that of certain objects which have been *always conjoined* together.' Induction, by a process of simple enumeration, has no logical force. All swans had been white, before the discovery in Hume's time of black swans in Australia. Swans had not been necessarily white, any more than a flame necessarily caused gunpowder to explode.

There are many difficulties in Hume's approach, and these are not just limited to common sense. How can we possibly carry on living, if this is all we know for certain? Hume was well aware of this objection to his philosophy. 'When we leave our closet, and engage in the common affairs of life, its conclusions seem to vanish, like the phantoms of the night on the appearance of morning; and it is difficult for us to retain even that conviction, which we had attain'd with difficulty.' What in fact Hume was pointing out was the utter precariousness of the human condition with regard to knowledge. We *think* we know a great deal – but in reality much of what we think we know is mere supposition. Reliable supposition, but supposition nonetheless.

This position is strangely similar to the state of knowledge today, when the ultimate truths of science have long since departed the realms of credibility or common sense. We grudgingly accept the truths of science, which would have us believe that a torrent of subatomic particles streams through our solid earth, shadows of anti-matter dog our every step, and a curve-ball of space would carry us into the past. Yet we continue to live our lives in a Newtonian universe, with ripe apples falling by gravity onto the cosy lawns of reality. Today the high ground of what we are assured is the truth is no less nonsensical than in Hume's philosophy. Yet as ever the laughably inadequate notions of common sense continue to suffice.

Despite Hume's destruction of the basis for all science, he had the highest regard for Newton and his experimental approach. Indeed, Hume's notion of impressions may well have been inspired by a passage from Newton's *Optics* about light rays and objects: 'In them there is nothing else than a certain power and disposition to stir up a sensation of this or that colour.' (In other words, we don't experience the object itself.) Hume had the deepest admiration for science, especially for the rigour of its methods. He felt sure that this was the way forward to a better future. Yet, paradoxically, Hume's philosophy plunges humanity back into the past – to a position which it hadn't occupied since the Middle Ages. Copernicus had displaced humanity and the earth from the centre of the Universe. Hume's solipsist empiricism firmly re-established humanity at the centre of whatever was going on (though in Hume's case this didn't actually include the earth, let alone the Universe).

Hume's position has many interesting anomalies. Berkeley had relied upon God to prop up the world when we weren't looking. With Hume, there was no world to prop up. And if there are no such things as corporeal bodies, continuity, or cause and effect, there is hardly room for God. Hume may not have believed in God, but his philosophy reduces us to a situation remarkably close to that of certain Buddhist mystics. Where Berkeley had reduced philosophy to a joke, Hume explained the joke (away). However, this was unlikely to induce people take it any more seriously.

In 1739 Hume returned to Britain and published his *Treatise*. He then sat back, waiting for the savage and vitriolic attacks that would inevitably appear from the critics – to which he would reply with consummate brilliance, thus guaranteeing him fame, money, public notoriety, the widespread approbation of poets and financiers, the love of fair women and financiers' wives, and all the other little marks of recognition that any tyro philosopher comes to expect as his due. Sadly, this was not to be. Hume's great masterpiece 'fell dead-born from the press', as he put it. His work suffered the worst fate of all: no one noticed it. And Hume's reaction? 'Being naturally of a cheerful and sanguine temper, I very soon recovered from the blow.' He returned to Edinburgh and began writing essays on moral and political topics. These achieved some recognition, and in 1744 he put himself forward as candidate for the Chair of Moral Philosophy at Edinburgh University. Unfortunately, it appeared that at least one person had after all read his *Treatise of Human Nature*. A vehement objection was lodged against Hume's candidature, citing his *Treatise* and claiming that it was a work of heresy and atheism. These were difficult charges to deny, especially to someone who had evidently read the book. (Hume's earlier intention to dazzle the outraged critics with his brilliant ripostes had presumably been based on the assumption that these critics wouldn't take the unprecedented step of actually reading his work.) Hume wasn't given the job at his old university, and left Edinburgh in disgust.

Hume decided to look for a job more suited to his abilities. Eventually he was offered the post of tutor to the mad Marquess of Anandale at his home near St Albans. This appeared to fit the bill, and Hume accepted.

During the periods when his lordship was beyond even philosophic instruction (which appears to have been considered as a last resort) Hume started to write a *History of England*, but soon became so dispirited that he gave up, promising himself that he would return to this project later.

The country too was now in the grip of its own insanity – namely, the 1745 Jacobite Rebellion. A Scottish army of 5,000 men successfully invaded England, then retreated in embarrassment, finally to be massacred at the Battle of Culloden. Luckily for Hume he was in England throughout the rebellion, and was thus able to observe it with some detachment. A number of his friends in Edinburgh were forced to take sides, with unfortunate consequences. Hume's dry comment on the affair was 'Eight millions of people [might] have been subdued and reduced to slavery by five thousand, the bravest, but still the most worthless amongst them.'

This episode had a profound effect on Hume. He had seen history unfolding around him, even if he hadn't been directly involved in it. This deficiency was soon remedied when he was sacked from the job of tutoring a lunatic, and forced to lower his sights still further by becoming secretary to a general.

General James St Clair was waiting to set off on a military expedition against the French in Canada when he took on his new secretary. The ships and the army for this expedition had all been assembled at Portsmouth for several months. But the Secretary of State, the Duke of Newcastle, couldn't make up his mind about precisely what to do with them. This was the man, of whom it was said that he lost half an hour every morning, and spent the rest of the day looking for it. Against some stiff competition, this period is frequently judged as the most incompetent in British military history: ideal subject matter for our budding philosophical historian, who was now on hand to witness for himself the wonder of the military mind at work.

The Duke of Newcastle finally found his lost half hour and ordered General St Clair's expedition to put to sea and attack the French – not in Canada, but in France. When General St Clair asked the Duke what they were expected to do with the specially selected and trained American Indian trackers they had on board, this question was dismissed as irrelevant. The general then asked *where* in France he was expected to launch his attack, and was told that anywhere would do. General St Clair (together with his new secretary) caught the stagecoach back to Portsmouth and went on board the expedition's flagship. Here the general discovered a problem. No one on any of the ships had a map of France. Hume advanced the information that he knew what it looked like, and could even draw a sketch if the general wished. But in the end an officer was sent ashore to see if they had anything in the local bookshop. He came back with a secondhand book about France, which happened to have a small map in the back. Hume confirmed that it was definitely the right shape, and the general set sail for France – having been informed that he couldn't miss it, as long as he sailed due south.

The British fleet finally arrived off l'Orient (whose position on the south-west coast of Brittany, i.e. not facing Britain, suggests that General St Clair may initially have succeeded in missing France). Just along the coast from l'Orient the general landed his army (while Hume avidly took notes for his projected *History of England*). The general's aim was to besiege the important naval harbour at l'Orient, but unfortunately soon after he landed it began to rain. His 3,000 troops had been cooped up on board their ships for months, and began suffering from cramp as they marched through the mud. In the end, they couldn't even stand upright. (Common sense suggests that something a little stronger than rainwater may have contributed to this condition.) Meanwhile inside l'Orient the French discovered that they outnumbered the British invaders by seven to one. The two opposing forces exchanged a few rounds of cannon fire, and the military geniuses on either side then retired to ponder the situation over dinner.

The British high command soon came to the conclusion that their legless troops were better off on board ship, and marched them back under cover of darkness. Meanwhile the French commander, for reasons which only an expert military mind could possibly comprehend, had decided to surrender. When the large French force arrived to surrender next morning, they discovered a few disconsolate British artillery men whom everyone seemed to have forgotten about, sheltering from the rain beside their dripping guns. The French now found themselves with a superiority of nearly five thousand to one. Wisely realizing that the sheer logistics of having to accept the surrender of so many men was obviously beyond these few ridiculous Britishers, the French changed their tactics and took the Britishers prisoner. Meanwhile the British fleet and its philosopher-in-residence got lost in a storm, and after various adventures they all sailed home to collect their medals.

As a result of this glorious campaign General St Clair was rewarded with the leadership of an important diplomatic mission to Vienna and Turin. He set off, accompanied by his secretary and a staff of diplomatic advisers.

Hume reacted variously to his travels through Europe. 'Germany is . . . full of industrious honest People, & were it united it would be the greatest Power that ever was in the world,' he noted perceptively. 'The common People are here, almost every where, much better treated & more at their Ease, than in France; and not very much inferior to the English, notwithstanding all the Airs the latter give themselves.' However, he wasn't quite so impressed by the Austrians in Styria: 'as much as the Country is agreeable in its Wildness; as much are the Inhabitants savage & deform'd & monstrous in their Appearance. Very many of them have ugly swelld Throats: Idiots and Deaf People swarm in every Village; and the general Aspect of the People is the most shocking I ever saw. One wou'd think, that as this was the great Road, thro which all the barbarous Nations made their Irruptions into the Roman Empire, they always left here the Refuse of their Armies before they enterd into the Enemies Country.' Hume's reaction was not just an attack of spleen occasioned by the tiresome and enervating rigours of stagecoach travel through the Alps. His observations were no exaggeration, even if his diagnosis was wide of the mark. It's now known that this region suffered from an iodine deficiency in the diet, resulting in widespread goitre and lunacy.

But the locals weren't the only ones to suffer from mental derangement. When the mission reached Turin, Hume fell ill. A fellow member of the mission recorded: 'He was affected by a most violent Fever, attended with its natural Symptoms, Delerium and Ravings. In the Paroxisms of his Disorder he often talked, with much seeming Perturbation, of the Devil, of Hell, and of Damnation, and one night, while his Nursetender happened to be asleep, He rose from his Bed, and made towards a deep Well, which was in the Court-yard, with a Design, as was supposed, to drown himself, but, finding the Back Door Locked, He rushed into a room where, upon a Couch, the Gentlemen of the Family were, He well knew, used to deposit their Swords, and here he was found by the Servants who had been awakened by the noise He had made at the door in endeavouring to open it, and was by them forcibly brought back to his Bed.'

Hume appears to have quickly recovered,

and this 'whimsical Adventure' became a source of merriment amongst the company. Though Hume took a more sober view of it, remonstrating: 'Do you suppose Philosophy to be proof against Madness? The Organisation of my Brain was impaired, and I was as mad as any Man in Bedlam.' Hume seems to have been fully aware of, and to have feared, his largely latent mental disorder. And we can only speculate about its possible effect on his intellectual activities. Though it's intriguing that such a thorough-going atheist should reveal manic fears of the devil, hell and damnation. Likewise, one can only wonder how many other similar episodes took place, which are not recorded. There are many important questions here, which will probably never be answered.

General St Clair and his secretary eventually brought their mission to a successful conclusion, having travelled all around Europe and achieved nothing. (It's the achievements

in this field which usually spell disaster.)
Hume then decided that he'd had enough.
Having educated a madman and served as
secretary to a general, he now felt himself suit-
ably qualified to re-enter the philosophic fray.
He returned to Edinburgh, where he set about
rewriting his great philosophic flop. The first
part he turned into *An Enquiry Concerning
Human Understanding*, the work which was
to spread his ideas throughout Europe. The
last part he turned into *An Enquiry Concerning the Principles of Morals*, which he always
mistakenly believed to be his finest work.

It may be difficult for some to see how a
philosophical solipsist, who had exploded the
notion of cause and effect, continuity and even
bodies, could embark upon a moral philosophy. But where ethics is concerned, Hume
chooses to ignore the conclusions of his
thoroughgoing empiricism. Though he does
relate his ethics to the structure of his empiricism. Thus passions observed in others are

received as impressions. Compassion, on the other hand, begins as an idea, but if it is sufficiently strong and lively can become an impression. As one would expect from Hume's temperament, his moral philosophy is essentially humane. Compassion, or sympathy, is seen as the basis of all moral qualities. This brings personal happiness as well as social benefit. Hume esteems moral qualities according to their usefulness or their agreeableness – with regard to the individual and the community. These ideas had developed from the democratic liberalism of Locke, which placed emphasis on a social contract guaranteeing citizens natural rights under the law. Hume's ideas were to have a formative influence on the nineteenth-century Utilitarians, such as Bentham and Mill, who developed them into the formula: 'the greatest happiness of the greatest number'. However, this laudable wish for social happiness had an inherent flaw. What of the scapegoat whose public hanging will give so much joy to the majority of the populace? Reducing public morality to a mathematical equation, with the majority carrying the day on all matters, leaves minorities vulnerable to discrimination.

In 1752 Hume was made Keeper of the Advocates' Library in Edinburgh. This far from onerous employment gave him the opportunity to write more philosophical essays on a wide variety of subjects. The essay was all the rage at the time as the latest fashionable literary form. Although Hume was not so brilliant stylistically as Addison and Steele, his ideas were more profound. The topics of his essays range from disparate subjects such as politics and standards of public taste, through analogous topics such as tragedy and marriage, to subjects as similar as polygamy and stoicism. His essays on economic topics included many formative ideas in this embryo pseudo-science. And his essays on miracles (no such thing) and suicide (up to you) were to cause a sensation when they were finally published.

As a result of his employment with General St Clair, Hume had now seen first-hand what history was all about. Heartened by this insight he decided to embark once more upon his *History of England*. This begins with the invasion of Julius Caesar in 55 BC, and ends with the Glorious Revolution of 1688. Hume finally finished his history in 1762, having progressed at the rate of a century a year, the same rate as Gibbon claimed whilst writing his *Decline and Fall of the Roman Empire* which was published four years later. Hume's *History* was ranked as second only to Gibbon's masterpiece, but consistently outsold it and remained a bestseller for almost a century (until Macaulay's *History* became the standard work).

Hume's *History of England* is very readable, and was one of the first to broaden its scope by including the cultural and scientific interests of the period. Because it refused to subscribe to contemporary prejudices, it was immediately labelled as hopelessly biased. Hume's cultural comments strike me as being very fair. He spoke of the poets of the previous century producing 'monuments of genius perverted by indecency and bad taste, but none more than Dryden . . . both by reason of the greatness of his talents and the gross abuse he made of them'. And his philosophical views often obtrude to fine effect: 'While Newton seemed to draw off the veil from some of the mysteries of nature, he showed at the same time the imperfections of the mechanised philosophy; and thereby restored her ultimate secrets to that obscurity, in which they ever did and ever will remain.'

A year after Hume published this book he was honoured by having all his works placed on the Roman Catholic Index of banned books. In the centuries prior to our era, this accolade was very similar to the Nobel Prize.

It concentrated on genuine scientific, humanitarian and literary achievements, but was occasionally extended to charlatans or harmless mediocrities for political reasons.

In 1763 Hume was appointed secretary to the British ambassador in France. (The war so successfully waged by the likes of General St Clair and the commander of the garrison at l'Orient had eventually been called to a halt by the forces of sanity.) Hume's appointment in Paris was a huge success. He was now regarded as the British Voltaire, and was lionized by fashionable society. The ambassador quickly realized that his secretary's presence on the salon circuit was worth far more to promote British interests than anything else the embassy could offer, and encouraged him to attend as many parties as possible.

By now Hume was a repulsive figure. He was bloated and red in the face, ate too much, enjoyed his drink, and was generally rather clumsy. But he was also very intelligent and had a fine droll wit. The French had never seen anything like this before. To them, elegance and wit were virtually synonymous. For one to appear, without a semblance of the other, was a truly British eccentricity. Owing to Hume's extreme ungainliness, he was even excused from bowing at Court; and after one hilarious disaster was also no longer required to make his exit walking backwards towards the door. Hume was presented to the King and all the members of his family – even his young grandchildren, who each had to memorize a little speech in honour of 'M'sieur Yoome' and how they were looking forward to reading his *History of England*.

Despite Hume's appearance and enjoyment of social occasions he was not exactly a happy man. Inwardly he kept a tight rein on his emotions. He enjoyed the company of women, but privately characterized himself as 'a gallant who gives no offence to husbands and lovers'. Yet all this lionizing caused him momentarily to drop his guard. When he encountered a beautiful intelligent woman, who indicated that she was attracted to him physically, he quickly fell for her.

But this was France, where such things are never simple. The Comtesse de Boufflers was the mistress of the Prince de Conti, one of the most powerful political figures in the land. She was thirty-eight, and Hume was fifty-two. They quickly became friends, but were both wary of any further involvement. They corresponded with one another, using the elaborate manners of the period as a subtle, devious and often flimsy disguise for their true emotions. Hume told her: 'You have saved me from a total indifference towards every thing in human life.' But in the end it seems they were both afraid of each other, and each became convinced of the futility of the situation. Nothing came of it, and when Hume returned to England in 1765 they never met again. Yet they did continue to correspond, and the last letter we have in Hume's hand is addressed to his understanding countess.

It was the Comtesse de Boufflers who was instrumental in Hume meeting Jean-Jacques Rousseau, the great French political theorist and philosopher. Nowadays it's customary to characterize Rousseau as a madman and a bastard (in the pejorative sense), whose ideas led directly to social evil of the worst kind. And there's no denying this case. Rousseau was mentally unstable; he personally delivered, one by one, all five of his infant children by his mistress to the foundlings' home down the street; and his ideas encourage uncivilized behaviour. He believed that true virtue lay in the 'noble savage' who was uncorrupted by civilization. He was against a social contract which guaranteed natural rights, and in favour of diktat by the 'general will'. This he felt was bound to be directed towards the common good, and when the individual voluntarily subjected himself to it, he would be 'forced to be free'. Inevitably, this has an ominous ring to twentieth-century ears. Rousseau's ideas were to inspire both the glories and the excesses of the French Revolution, and continued to play a similar role in the twentieth century. His ideas are recognizable in Fascism and Communism, as well as the underlying drift towards self-expression and liberalism.

But the Rousseau who met Hume was more than just a time-bomb of explosive ideas. As a man he is best understood as the genius who inspired the Romantic Movement, and personally as a sort of walking naked sensibility. He was the precise opposite of Hume, both temperamentally and philosophically. And yet they were both on the same side. They both strove for reform. The old Europe of absolute monarchs and the landed gentry was beginning to give way to a more communal urban society, with liberal democratic tendencies. A process of evolution had started with Descartes, and progressed with the rise of the introspective novel. Europe was witnessing the advent of a widespread self-consciousness: the birth of an individuality which thought for itself. Rousseau's concern was with the individuality itself, its expression and self-realization. Hume was concerned with the condition of thinking for oneself, and seeing the world through eyes cleansed of the old preconceptions. For him there was no such thing as a soul, no one had ever perceived a 'mind', we experienced no causality or God. Rousseau, on the other hand, produced no coherent philosophy, but will be remembered for ever for such resonant ideas as 'the noble savage' and 'the general will'.

Rousseau was on the run (after publishing *Emile*, which denied the divine right of kings and supported democracy), and Hume offered to look after him. Unfortunately, by the time Rousseau arrived in England he had been driven insane by his persecutors. He would embrace Hume, saying how much he loved him; but within no time he would become convinced that Hume was in league with his enemies and plotting against him. Hume did his best, Rousseau did his worst. To everyone's relief, Rousseau eventually fled to France – where he began spreading all kinds of slanders against Hume. The philosopher had met the genius, and neither had understood the other. The nature of their meeting was ominously symbolic – the struggle between their two positions continues to this day.

In 1769 Hume returned to live in Edinburgh. By now he was enormous. 'The fattest of Epicurus's hogs', according to Gibbon, who was no lightweight himself (his comment on Hume was intended as approbation). Hume continued to work hard, revising and rewriting his *History* and his philosophical works, and writing essays. He also wrote an oddly objective and evasive brief autobiography. Perhaps he didn't want to give ammunition to his enemies – who were many. To the conservative elements of the establishment, the Church, orthodox academia, etc., he remained anathema. On the other hand, an anonymous pamphlet called 'Character of — by himself' which was certainly about Hume, and almost certainly by him, contains deep insights into his character and self-assessment. 'A very good man the constant purpose of whose life is to do mischief.' 'An enthusiast without religion, a philosopher who despairs to attain the truth.' 'Exempt from vulgar prejudices, full of his own.'

Hume now became the famous old man of Edinburgh. He enjoyed dining at length with his friends, who became known as the 'Eater-ati'. But he also continued to discus his ideas with his intellectual peers – such as his long-term friend Adam Smith, the social philosopher and pioneering theoretical economist. Hume and Smith shared many ideas on social philosophy, and it has been suggested that

Hume even influenced Smith in his theory that the interests of society are best guided by the 'invisible hand' of competition. This hand, which shaped the twentieth century, looks set to throttle the twenty-first when there will be strictly limited resources for which to compete – but neither Hume nor Smith should be held responsible for the blindness of present-day economists. They lived at the dawning of the era of seemingly unlimited possibilities (in so many spheres), an era on which the sun is now fast setting.

But in other respects Hume's ideas are often in deep accord with those of the twentieth century. 'If we take in our hand any volume – of divinity or school metaphysics, for instance – let us ask: "Does it contain any abstract reasoning concerning quantity or number?" No. "Does it contain any experimental reasoning concerning matter of fact and existence?" No. Commit it then to the flames, for it can contain nothing but sophistry and illusion.' And: 'The whole world presents nothing but the idea of a blind Nature . . . pouring forth from her lap, without discernment or parental care, her maimed and abortive children.' Such opinions were a rarity in the mid eighteenth century.

Gradually Hume's physique and lifestyle began to take their toll. He became increasingly ill, and eventually two eminent surgeons were called in to examine him. One after the other they prodded their fingers and squeezed his massive stomach; in the end they agreed that he was suffering from a tumour of the liver. Ever the bold but sceptical seeker after truth, Hume prodded his own fingers into his stomach, and personally confirmed their diagnosis, discovering a tumour 'about the Bigness of an Egg', which was 'flat and round'.

His health gradually began to fail, and he lost a lot of weight. Word got around that Hume was dying, and people flocked from far and wide to see if the great atheist would repent on his deathbed. Boswell arrived to find that Hume was 'lean, ghastly and quite of an earthy appearance'. (It's difficult to decide whether this last remark is inexact or profound.) But when Boswell asked Hume if he believed it was possible there was an afterlife, 'He answered It was possible a piece of coal put on the fire would not burn.'

At the end of a long illness, Hume finally died on 25 August 1776 (without repenting). A considerable crowd gathered outside his door to watch the funeral procession of 'the Atheist'; but he was not an unpopular figure with the mob, only the Church. And unlike the great philosophers to come, his philosophy remains plausible. But there's one snag. When we read Hume's philosophy we recognize that we think like this – but we know that we don't live like this. Is it possible that this time philosophy was right, and that *we* are the ones who are wrong?

Afterword

Epistemology, the study of how we acquire knowledge, was seen by many as the core of philosophy. Prior to Hume, epistemology had been a thriving industry, producing all kinds of theories. Upon these were based the amazing systems which were the pride and joy of philosophy. This was philosophy's main selling point: a system which explained *everything*. With Hume, the bottom fell out of the market. Hume showed that the construction of philosophical systems was no longer possible. However, it is in the nature of philosophy to attempt the impossible. In the era immediately following Hume, German philosophers were to produce the greatest philosophical systems known to man.

Kant read Hume, and claimed that this experience 'awoke me from my dogmatic slumbers'. As a result he produced an all-embracing system of the highest ingenuity and insight. This in turn was followed by Hegel, who produced the greatest philosophical dinosaur of them all – a metaphysical system so vast and complex as to be well beyond the comprehension of mere mortals. It was Nietzsche who saw that these misguided attempts could only produce extinct beasts. In Nietzsche's view, there 'was more sense in a page of Hume that in the entire works of Hegel'.

Yet even Nietzsche failed to clear the epistemological hurdle which Hume had placed in the way of philosophic advance – admitting that Hume's objections (to almost everything) were unanswerable. The only way to proceed was to ignore them. We had to continue to philosophize regardless – just as we continued to live regardless of Hume's demolition of continuity, causality, etc. There were always lots of other things to philosophize about.

In the twentieth century Wittgenstein adopted a comparable approach. Cavalierly ignoring Hume (to the point of not even bothering to read him), Wittgenstein soon arrived at a remarkably similar philosophic situation. (Great minds don't always think alike because they plagiarize the same sources.)

Hume may well have pushed Humpty-Dumpty from the wall, but still nobody has worked out how to put him together again. Nowadays philosophy insists upon ignoring certain questions (which it deems unanswerable). It's worth noting that it also ignores certain answers.

Key quotations

All the perceptions of the human mind resolve themselves into two distinct kinds, which I shall call IMPRESSIONS and IDEAS. The differences betwixt these consists in the degrees of force and liveliness, with which they strike our mind, and make their way into our thought or consciousness. Those perceptions, which enter with most force and violence, we may name *impressions*; and under this name I comprehend all our sensations, passions and emotions, as they make their first appearances in the soul. By *ideas* I mean the faint images of these in thinking and reasoning; such as, for instance, are all the perceptions excited by the present discourse, excepting only, those which arise from the sight and touch, and

excepting the immediate pleasure or unease it may occasion.
A Treatise of Human Nature (ed. L. Selby-Bigge), Book 1, page 1.

There is another division of our perceptions, which it will be convenient to observe, and which extends itself both to our impressions and ideas. The division is into SIMPLE and COMPLEX. Simple perceptions or impressions and ideas are such that admit of no distinction or separation. The complex are the contrary to these, and may be distinguished into two parts. Tho' a particular colour, taste and smell are qualities all united together in this apple, 'tis easy to perceive they are not the same, but are at least distinguishable from each other . . . *all our simple ideas in their first appearances are deriv'd from simple impressions, which*

are correspondent to them, and which they
exactly represent.

> *A Treatise of Human Nature,*
> Book 1, page 2

Thus not only our reason fails us in the discovery of the *ultimate connexion* of causes and effects, but even after experience has inform'd us of their *constant conjunction*, 'tis impossible for us to satisfy ourselves by our reason, why we shou'd extend that experience beyond those particular instances, which have fallen under our observation. We suppose, but we are never able to prove, that there must be a resemblance betwixt those objects, of which we have had experience, and those which lie beyond the reach of our discovery.

> *A Treatise of Human Nature,*
> Book 1, page 91

We may well ask, *What causes induce us*

to believe in the existence of body? but 'tis vain to ask, *Whether there be body or not?* That is a point, which we must take for granted in all our reasonings . . . We ought to examine apart these two questions, which are commonly confounded together, *viz.* Why we attribute a CONTINU'D existence to objects, even when they are not present to the senses; and why we suppose them to have an existence DISTINCT from the mind. Under this last head I comprehend their situation as well as relations, their *external* position as well as the *independence* of their existence and operation . . . The senses give us no notion of continued existence, because they cannot operate beyond the extent, in which they really operate. They as little produce the opinion of a distinct existence, because they neither can offer it to the mind as represented, nor as original. To offer it as represented, they must present both an object and an image.

To make it appear as original, they must convey a falsehood; and this falsehood must lie in the relations and situation: In order to which they must be able to compare the object with ourselves; and even in that case they do not, nor is it possible they shou'd, deceive us. We may, therefore, conclude with certainty, that the opinion of a continu'd and a distinct existence never arises from the senses.

A Treatise of Human Nature,
Book 1, pages 187, 188, 191

Whatever convincing arguments philosophers may fancy they can produce to establish the belief of objects independent of the mind, 'tis obvious these objects are known but to very few, and that 'tis not by them, that children, peasants, and the greater part of mankind are induc'd to attribute objects to some impressions, and deny them to others. Accordingly we find, that all the conclusions, which the vulgar form on this head, are directly contrary to those, which are confirm'd by philosophy. For philosophy informs us, that every thing, which appears to the mind, is nothing but a perception, and is interrupted, and dependent on the mind; whereas the vulgar confound perceptions and objects, and attribute a distinct continu'd existence to the very things they feel or see. This sentiment, then, as it is entirely unreasonable, must proceed from some faculty other than the understanding. To which we may add, that as long as we take our perceptions and objects to be the same, we can never infer the existence of the one from that of the other, nor form any argument from the relation of cause and effect; which is the only one that can assure us of matter of fact. Even after we distinguish our perceptions from our objects, 'twill appear presently, that we are still incapable of reasoning from the existence of one to that of the other: So that upon the whole our reason neither does, nor is it possible it ever shou'd, upon any supposition, give us an assurance of the continu'd and distinct existence of body. That opinion must be entirely owing to the IMAGINATION.

A Treatise of Human Nature,
Book 1, page 193

Errors in religion are dangerous; those in philosophy only ridiculous.

A Treatise of Human Nature,
Book 2, page 272

Reason is, and ought only to be the slave of the passions, and can never pretend to any other office than to serve and obey them.

A Treatise on Human Nature,
Book 2, page 415

What philosophical truths can be more advantageous to society, than those here delivered, which represent virtue in all her genuine and most engaging charms, and makes us approach her with ease, familiarity, and affection? The dismal dress falls off, with which many divines, and some philosophers, have covered her; and nothing appears but gentleness, humanity, beneficience, affability; nay, even at proper intervals, play, frolic, and gaiety. She talks not of useless austerities and rigours, suffering and self-denial. She declares that her sole purpose is to make her votaries and all mankind, during every instant of their existence, if possible, cheerful and happy; nor does she ever willingly part with any pleasure but in hopes of ample compensation in some other period of their lives. The sole trouble which she demands is that of just calculation, and a steady preference of the greater happiness. And if any austere pretenders approach her, enemies of joy and pleasure, she either rejects them as hypocrites and deceivers; or, if she admit them in her train, they are ranked, however, among the least favoured of her votaries.

An Enquiry Concerning the Principles of Morals (ed. Selby-Bigge) p. 280

I have often observed, that, among the French, the first questions with regard to a stranger are, *Is he polite? Has he wit?* In our own country, the chief praise bestowed is always that of a *good-natured, sensible fellow*.

An Enquiry Concerning the Principles of Morals, p. 262

Were the disposal of human life so much reserved as the peculiar province of the Almighty, that it were an encroachment on his life for men to dispose of their own lives, it would be equally criminal to act for the preservation of life as for its destruction. If I turn aside a stone which is falling upon my head, I disturb the course of nature; and I invade the peculiar province of the Almighty, by lengthening out my life beyond the period, which, by the general laws of matter and motion, he has assigned it.

A hair, a fly, an insect, is able to destroy this mighty being whose life is of such importance. Is it an absurdity to suppose that human prudence may lawfully dispose of what depends on such insignificant causes?

It would be no crime in me to divert the *Nile* or *Danube* from its course, were I able to effect such purposes. Where then is the crime of turning a few ounces of blood from their natural channels!

On Suicide. Essays (ed. Copley)
p. 320

The powers of men are no more superior to their wants, considered merely in this life, than those of foxes and hares are, compared to *their* wants and to *their* period of existence.

On the Immortality of the Soul. Essays (ed. Copley), p. 326

Our insensibility before the composition of the body seems to natural reason a proof of a like state after dissolution.

On the Immortality of the Soul. Essays (ed. Copley), p. 330

In Newton this island may boast of having produced the greatest and rarest genius that ever rose for the ornament and instruction of the species. Cautious in admitting no principles but such as were founded on experiment, but resolute to adopt every such principle, however new or unusual; from modesty, ignorant of his superiority above the rest of mankind, and thence less careful to accommodate his reasonings to common apprehensions; more anxious to merit than acquire fame; he was, from these causes, long unknown to the world. But his reputation at last broke out with a lustre which scarcely any writer, during his own lifetime, had ever before attained . . .

Most of the celebrated writers of this age remain monuments of genius perverted by indecency and bad taste; and none more than Dryden, both by reason of the greatness of his talents and the gross abuse which he made of them. His plays, excepting a few scenes, are utterly disfigured by vice or folly, or both; his translations appear too much the offspring of haste and hunger; even his fables are ill-chosen tales, conveyed in an incorrect though spirited versification. Yet, amid this great number of loose productions, the refuse of our language, there are found some small pieces – his Ode to St Cecilia, the greater part of Absalom and Achitophel, and a few more – which discover so great genius, such richness of expression, such pomp and variety of numbers, that they leave us equally full of regret and indignation on account of the inferiority, or, rather, great absurdity, of his other writings.

The History of England (ed. Kilcup),
ch. 71: 'The Reign of James II,
pages 281, 282

Look round this universe. What an immense profusion of beings, animated and organised, sensible and active! You admire this prodigious variety and fecundity. But inspect a little more narrowly these living existences, the only beings worth regarding. How hostile and destructive to each other! How insufficient all of them for their own happiness! How contemptible or odious to the spectator! The whole represents nothing but the idea of a blind nature, impregnated by a great vivifying principle, and pouring forth from her lap, without discernment or parental care, her maimed and abortive children.

Dialogues concerning Natural Religion (ed. Kemp Smith), page 174

Chronology of significant philosophical dates

6th century BC — The start of western philosophy with Thales of Miletus.

end of 6th century BC — Death of Pythagoras.

399 BC — Socrates sentenced to death in Athens.

c387 BC — Plato founds the Academy in Athens, the first university.

335 BC — Aristotle founds the Lyceum in Athens, rival school to the Academy.

324 AD — Emperor Constantine moves capital of Roman Empire to Byzantium.

400 AD — St Augustine writes his

	Confessions. Philosophy absorbed into Christian theology.
410 AD	Sack of Rome by Visigoths.
529 AD	Closure of Academy in Athens by Emperor Justinian marks end of Greco-Roman era and start of Dark Ages.
mid 13th Century	Thomas Aquinas writes his commentaries on Aristotle. Era of Scholasticism.
1453	Fall of Byzantium to Turks, end of Byzantine Empire.
1492	Columbus reaches America. Renaissance in Florence and revival of interest in Greek learning.
1543	Copernicus publishes *De revolutionibus orbium caelestium* (*On the Revolution of the Celestial Orbs*) proving

mathematically that the earth revolves around the sun.

1633   Galileo forced by Church to recant heliocentric theory of the universe.

1641   Descartes publishes his *Meditations*, the start of modern philosophy.

1677   Death of Spinoza allows publication of his *Ethics*.

1687   Newton publishes *Principia*, introducing concept of gravity.

1689   Locke publishes *Essay Concerning Human Understanding*. Start of Empiricism.

1710   Berkeley publishes *Principles of Human Knowledge*, advancing Empiricism to new extremes.

1716   Death of Leibnitz.

1739–40   Hume publishes *Treatise of Human Nature*, taking Empiricism to its logical limits.

1781   Kant, woken from his 'dogmatic slumbers' by Hume, publishes *Critique of Pure Reason*. Great era of German metaphysics begins.

1807   Hegel publishes *The Phenomenology of Mind*: high point of German metaphysics.

1818   Schopenhauer publishes *The World as Will and Representation*, introducing Indian philosophy into German metaphysics.

1889   Nietzsche, having declared 'God is dead', succumbs to madness in Turin.

1921   Wittgenstein publishes *Tractatus-Logico-*

Philosophicus, claiming the 'final solution' to the problems of philosophy.

1920s   Vienna Circle propound Logical Positivism.

1927   Heidegger publishes *Sein und Zeit* (*Being and Time*), heralding split between analytical and continental philosophy.

1943   Sartre publishes *L'être et le néant* (*Being and Nothingness*), advancing Heidegger's thought and instigating Existentialism.

1953   Posthumous publication of Wittgenstein's *Philosophical Investigations*. High era of Linguistic Analysis.